GALATIA

Lycaonia

ASIA

Phrygia

Pisidia

■ Iconium

■ Lystra

Derbe ■

Tarsus

PAMPHYLIA

CILICIA

LYCIA

Antioch ■

SYRIA

CYPRUS

PHENICIA
(Phenice)

Damascus

*The Great Sea
(Mediterranean Sea)*

PALESTINE

Caesarea ■ Samaria

ARABIA

Joppa

Jerusalem

Lydda

N

W   E

S

*Other books and products
by the authors and illustrator:*

Jesus' Healings, Part 1

Jesus' Healings, Part 2

Jesus' Healings, Part 3

Ten Commandments Cards

Beatitudes Cards

Interactive Bible Time-Line

New Testament
Healings
Peter, Paul, and Friends

Written by

Mary Jo Beebe
Olene E. Carroll
Nancy H. Fischer

Illustrated by

Genevieve Meek

Table of Contents

GENERAL PUBLICATIONS
BIBLE PRODUCTS, CSPS
Boston, Massachusetts, U.S.A.

ISBN: 0-87510-408-8
© 2003 General Publications Bible Products, CSPS
All rights reserved
Printed in the United States of America

Introduction

About the Book

New Testament Healings is written for all ages—children, teenagers, and adults—anyone who is interested in the healing work of Jesus' followers.

Thirteen Healing Stories Included

This book brings to life in simple language the healing work of seven of Jesus' followers—Peter, John, Stephen, Philip, Ananias, Barnabas, and Paul. These works include healings of lameness, mental illness, paralysis, blindness, injuries, snakebite, and stomach disease as well as two accounts of restoring lives.

Stories Arranged in Chronological Order

The healings are in chronological order according to the book of Acts.

Stories—Self-Contained

Each of the healing stories in the book is self-contained, with references to other pages in the book for definitions and commentary. While this feature is helpful for reading and studying individual stories, we recommend that you take the time to read the book from beginning to end as well. This will give you a full and inspired understanding of the scope and importance of these healings.

Written in Simple Language

The stories are written in contemporary English and at a level young children can understand. Sidebars provide additional information and commentary about the stories that will be interesting to older children and adults. In a few of the stories, passages too difficult for young children to understand have been placed in sidebars.

While every attempt has been made to write the stories in simple language, some stories may still be beyond the understanding of very young children. Parents and teachers must use their own discretion about the appropriateness of stories. In some cases, it may be helpful to paraphrase a story or leave out certain sections.

Details and Ideas Added for Understanding

In writing the stories, we have added details and ideas with the intent of making the stories more understandable. The details are supported by authoritative Bible scholars. You can find sources in the bibliography on page 57.

Map Included with *New Testament Healings*

The book's map is printed on the inside front and back covers. In New Testament times, the lands around the Mediterranean Sea were made up of Roman regions, or provinces. The map shows the regions and cities in which Jesus' followers healed. It also shows other regions and cities referred to in the book. The names of these places are those used in the King James Version.

In some of the stories about Paul, *New Testament Healings* provides sidebars telling where he had traveled. These sidebars give the names of the regions only. It is helpful to note the general areas in which the Roman regions of New Testament times are located today: Illyricum is in Croatia; Macedonia and Achaia are in Greece; Asia, Lycia, Pamphylia, Galatia, and Cilicia are in Turkey; Arabia is in both Jordan and Saudi Arabia; Phenicia (also "Phenice" and spelled "Phoenicia" in many other versions of the Bible) is mostly in Lebanon today; Syria is mostly in Syria today; Italy is still called Italy; Melita is called Malta. "Palestine" is a term that was used for a region located in the general area of Israel today.

Stories Based on Concepts in the Bible

In the healing stories, we have identified spiritual truths that were the foundation of these healings. These truths are based on concepts found in translations of the Bible and in other writings.

See bibliography on page 57.

Introduction

Special Features of the Book

New Testament Healings includes features you may want to explore before you read the stories.

Understanding how the book is organized and arranged will enhance your enjoyment of it.

Bible book and verses where the story can be found.

Bible verses where other accounts of the story can be found.

Illustrations enhance children's (and adults') understanding and enjoyment of the stories.

The text is easily read and understood by all ages.

The end of each story is indicated by a large colored square.

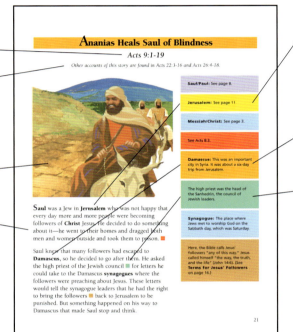

Sidebars like this show where information can be found in another story about a bolded word or phrase in this story.

Sidebars like this provide information about a bolded word or phrase in the story.

Sidebars like this provide commentary or information to expand on the text. The sidebar color matches a colored square in the story for easy reference.

NOTE: Bible quotations in sidebars are from the King James Version.

Bible verse sidebars provide a Bible verse with spiritual truths that Jesus' followers would have known—also comments about the practicality of these truths to heal today.

The "What Can YOU Do?" sidebars provide ideas for children and teens that help them see how they can apply the spiritual truths in the healing story to their lives.

Introduction

Christ Jesus—His Healing Legacy

At the beginning of Jesus' ministry, he announced his mission—to help and heal his fellow man. It happened in the synagogue in Nazareth on a Sabbath day. He read aloud from the prophet Isaiah—words that described his mission in life:

> *The Spirit of the Lord is upon me, because he hath anointed me to preach the gospel to the poor; he hath sent me to heal the brokenhearted, to preach deliverance to the captives, and recovering of sight to the blind, to set at liberty them that are bruised, to preach the acceptable year of the Lord (Luke 4:18,19).*

When he finished reading, Jesus told the people that this scripture was fulfilled that day. And then he began a three-year ministry that changed the lives of the people he met. Jesus was filled with spiritual power—with the Spirit of God—and this enabled him to heal people of illnesses and disabilities such as blindness, deafness, dumbness, leprosy, epilepsy, and paralysis and to restore people to life.

He sent his disciples out into the towns and villages to heal. And they returned, rejoicing that they had the power to heal, too. These humble men had the great privilege of being with Jesus daily, listening to his inspiring words, and seeing his wonderful healing works. The spiritual power they saw and felt revealed more and more to them that the Christ was not an earthly king but Jesus' spiritual selfhood.

He promised that after he left them they too would be filled with the Spirit of God. This Holy Spirit would be with them forever. It would help them see their own Christ-like nature—and enable them to continue Jesus' healing ministry.

Messiah/Christ: The Hebrew word for "Messiah" and the Greek word for "Christ" mean "anointed"—chosen and dedicated—to save or deliver. Many Jews believed the Messiah of the Old Testament was a special anointed king from the family of David, who would come someday. This king, the "Son of David," would get rid of all their enemies and set up a kingdom that would last forever. Other Jews believed the Messiah would be a priest who would purify the way Israel worshiped God. And others saw that a prophet like Moses would come.

Jesus didn't think of himself as an earthly king. He saw his role as fulfilling the scripture to heal and teach and to bring to light the "kingdom of God"—the reign of harmony. He saw the Christ as his—and everyone's—spiritual selfhood. He knew that God created man in His image and likeness and kept him that way. Therefore, man is always spiritual, whole, and complete. Jesus never allowed the material picture of sickness, sin, and death to have power or reality in his thought. By knowing that the Christ, or his spiritual selfhood, was the only truth or reality, Jesus destroyed the "enemies" of sickness, sin, and death. And this understanding of the Christ brought the "kingdom of God"—complete harmony.

Jesus' life, teachings, and spiritual healings showed how clearly he understood his spiritual selfhood. People began to give him the title of "Christ," calling him "Christ Jesus." Christ Jesus is an example for us all. We, too, can heal as he commanded his followers to do, by understanding God's all-power and our spiritual relationship to Him.

Introduction

The Promise of the Holy Spirit and Healing

Jesus' followers knew that healing was expected of them. They had all been taught by the greatest spiritual healer the world has ever known. They had seen Jesus after he rose from the dead and could tell everyone that his resurrection had truly happened.

They knew that it was the Spirit that had enabled their Master to heal. And Jesus told them that they would receive this Holy Spirit—spiritual power—after he was gone. He also told them that this Spirit would be "another Comforter"—one that would always be by their side giving them good counsel. This Spirit of truth would lift their thoughts above what they saw with their eyes—what the apostle Paul later called "the flesh"—to the spiritual truth about God and His children. This truth was that God who is Spirit is good. He created His children in His likeness—spiritual and perfect—and He keeps them always in this state of love and perfection. With this understanding of God's great power within them, they would have all they needed to carry on Jesus' healing ministry.

After Jesus' resurrection, the followers—120 of them—met together in Jerusalem and prayed constantly. And then, on the day of Pentecost, they received the Holy Spirit—the spiritual power that Jesus had promised them. This Spirit was like a fire that couldn't be put out. It would be with them, and all of Jesus' followers, forever.

Holy Spirit: The Holy Spirit ("Holy Ghost" in the King James Version) refers to the Spirit of God that is always present and active in the lives of those who are willing to listen and turn to Him with their whole heart. The word "Holy" refers to what is Godlike. The Hebrew and Greek words for "Spirit" mean "wind" or "breath" and may refer to the life-giving activity of God, who inspires and creates.

In both the Old and New Testaments, the great leaders and prophets were filled with the Spirit of God, meaning their thoughts were filled with God and all that was spiritual and good. The Spirit of God was their source of strength and wisdom—their guidance and protection in times of trouble. Jesus brought an even higher understanding of the Spirit of God. He relied completely on God and His spiritual laws. These laws are all-powerful. When they are known and understood, the result in human life is freedom from limitation and evil of all kinds— of sin, sickness, and even death.

Jesus knew that God is the only power and presence and that He gives only good to His children. He knew that God is Spirit and that God created His children in his image and likeness. Jesus' thoughts were focused on the spiritual and not the material. He knew that God, Spirit, is life-giving, life-protecting. These spiritual laws were the "Holy Spirit" and were all-powerful—healing sin and sickness and restoring life. Jesus told his disciples that they would receive this Holy Spirit after he was gone (Acts 1:3-8). He referred to this Spirit as another "Comforter," to them—like "one called to the side of another" (John 14:16,17,26).

This image of the Holy Spirit right by their side must have been a great comfort to his followers. While he had been with them, they had depended on him for their spiritual understanding and support. But now, they would have another Comforter, also called the Spirit of truth (John 14:26), to guide them. Their thoughts would be filled with the spiritual laws of God. This would be a spiritual power that energized them and gave them all that they needed to continue Jesus' healing ministry.

Introduction

Healing by the Power of the Holy Spirit

After the day of Pentecost, Jesus' followers were filled with the Holy Spirit—with great spiritual power. And this power would enable them to heal. Nothing could stop them. Acts says that "many wonders and signs [healings] were done by the apostles" (Acts 2:43).

Thousands of people joined the followers, seeing the truth of their teachings and the proof through their healing works. The spiritual power that filled them was like a great light shining within their hearts and minds, giving them strength and energy and wisdom—and great joy in continuing Jesus' healing ministry.

In the Jerusalem area, Peter and John healed a man who had never walked. Then, people brought their sick into the streets for Peter to heal them, too. Stephen and Philip, two of the followers chosen by the apostles to help them with the growing needs of the church, healed numerous people. And Peter continued his healing mission in other cities, healing a paralyzed man and restoring a woman to life. A humble man in Damascus—Ananias—healed Paul and welcomed him into the company of Jesus' followers.

Paul and other followers took the healing power of the Holy Spirit into the far reaches of the Roman Empire. The book of Acts tells us that Paul healed a man of lameness, restored a young boy to life, healed a young girl of mental illness, healed a man of stomach illness, and healed himself of severe injuries and of a snakebite.

Reports of healing are found in the letters of Paul. He wrote to the followers in the city of Corinth in Achaia (Greece) listing the various gifts of the Holy Spirit that were blessing their church and the community. These gifts included "gifts of healing " (I Corinthians 12:7-11, 28-31).

After extensive travels to places like Arabia, Syria, Cyprus, Cilicia, Pamphylia, Pisidia and Lycaonia, Paul traveled to Jerusalem. There, he reported to the apostles that he and Barnabas had healed many people in these regions through the power of God (Acts 15:12).

Paul also wrote to the churches in Galatia reminding them of what they had learned about spiritual power and that the healings happening among them were through this power (Galatians 3:5).

At another time Paul wrote to the followers in Rome telling them of the healings he had done through the power of God all the way from Jerusalem to far-off Illyricum (Romans 15:18, 19).

The author of the book of Hebrews wrote about healings as if they were common knowledge in the early churches. He described the healings as varied and as a result of the power of God. And he explained that these healings showed the truth of the teachings of Jesus. He encouraged Jesus' followers not to put their faith into something that didn't have these kinds of healing proofs (Hebrews 2:1-4).

James, the brother of Jesus, who became a leader in the Jerusalem church, encouraged the followers to pray for the sick and told them that the prayer of faith would heal them (James 5:13-16).

Spiritual healing was accepted by Jesus' followers as a natural outcome of applying the spiritual laws of God that their Master had taught. No one was excluded from being a healer. Anyone who loved the Christ and whose thought was open and accepting of the Spirit of truth could heal. This is true today, too. Those who follow Jesus Christ in any age can know the great joy of spiritual healing!

Jesus' Followers and Their Healing Mission

Peter: Peter had been a fisherman, along with his brother Andrew, before Jesus selected him to be his disciple. Jesus often chose Peter, James, and John to be with him at times when he wanted these disciples to have special lessons. Peter was a bold, eager student, and Jesus gave him the name "Peter," which meant "rock." After Jesus was gone, Peter became a leader of the followers in Jerusalem. He was a "rock" of strength and faith, just as Jesus had said he would be. He was also a wonderful spiritual healer. Three of his individual healings are recorded in the Bible. At the gate of the Temple in Jerusalem, he and John healed a man who had never walked. He showed his great humility by giving credit to the power of God. When people in and around Jerusalem learned about this healing, they flocked to him to be healed. On travels outside the city, he healed a paralyzed man and restored a woman to life. Once, when he was arrested for teaching about Jesus, Peter boldly continued sharing the message of God's great power and love. And at another time when he was put in prison, he was freed through his prayers and those of other followers. Although Peter became known as the "apostle to the Jews," he once taught a Roman Centurion and his family and friends about Christ Jesus—and they became followers. The Bible says that they were filled with the Holy Spirit. This enthusiastic, faithful apostle did much to bring the message of the Christ to many people.

John: John and his older brother James were fishermen when Jesus chose them to become his disciples. John may have been the youngest of Jesus' disciples. Jesus singled out John, James, and Peter to be with him at special times such as at his transfiguration and at the raising of Jairus' daughter. John is traditionally known as the disciple whom Jesus loved. This disciple was the only one of Jesus' closest disciples who was at his crucifixion. Jesus showed his trust in this disciple by asking him to take care of his mother after he was gone. This disciple was also the first to believe in Jesus' resurrection. After Pentecost John and Peter healed a lame man at the Temple gate—the first recorded individual healing by apostles after Jesus' resurrection. John also taught in the Temple. He lived in Jerusalem for several years and became an important leader in the Jerusalem church, but he also traveled outside Jerusalem. When Philip was successful in healing and converting Samaritans, John and Peter were sent to help. Afterward, he and Peter preached in other places in Samaria.

Jesus' Followers and Their Healing Mission

Stephen: Many people had become Jesus' followers after the day of Pentecost. This increased the amount of work the apostles had to do. When they needed help distributing food to needy widows, they chose seven men for this work. Because Stephen was wise, had great faith in God, and was full of the Holy Spirit, he was one of those chosen. Stephen not only helped the widows but he also taught and healed many people. His teaching, however, was not accepted by everyone. The Jewish leaders even put him on trial. What he said when he defended himself made them even angrier. A mob gathered, picked up stones, and killed Stephen. His last words were a prayer for those who were stoning him, "Lord, do not blame them for this sin." Stephen's love and forgiveness must have made quite an impact on a young man who witnessed this scene—Saul of Tarsus.

Philip: This follower of Jesus was not Philip, one of Jesus' twelve closest disciples, but Philip, the evangelist. An evangelist is one who preaches the gospel—the good news about Jesus' life and teachings. Philip, who was wise and full of the Holy Spirit—the spiritual power of God—began his mission in Jerusalem where he was chosen to help the apostles in caring for needy widows. But after his coworker, Stephen, was killed, Philip left Jerusalem quickly to go to a city in Samaria. There he preached the good news and healed many people of illnesses, paralysis, and lameness. He brought much happiness to that city. Philip was always listening to God's direction. Once, the thought came to him to go to a lonely desert road, and he went—even though he didn't know what he would find. There a man from Ethiopia was traveling back to his home. Philip shared the good news about Jesus with this man, and he became a follower of Jesus Christ, too.

Ananias: The Bible says that Ananias was a "disciple." This probably means that he was a new follower of Jesus. He may have left Jerusalem and settled in Damascus because of the persecution of followers after Stephen's death. Ananias had a vision of Jesus Christ telling him to go to Saul, one of the worst persecutors, to heal him. In spite of doubts and fears, Ananias obeyed. He healed Saul of blindness and welcomed him as a new follower.

Jesus' Followers and Their Healing Mission

Barnabas: Barnabas was from the island of Cyprus. He was known as a very generous man because he sold his land and donated the money to Jesus' followers in Jerusalem. He also worked faithfully to spread the gospel message—the good news about Jesus' teachings. The apostles changed his name from Joseph to "Barnabas," meaning "son of encouragement" because of his kindness, gentleness, and remarkable ability to give people hope. When the apostles in Jerusalem were afraid to accept Saul as a new follower, Barnabas spoke to them and took away their fears. Later, Barnabas was sent to Antioch to help and encourage the new followers. And when the followers there needed an additional leader, Barnabas brought Saul. These two were then sent by the church to travel and share the message about Jesus Christ. When they returned to Jerusalem, they reported all their wonderful healings that had been done among the Gentiles. Later, Barnabas went on a mission with John Mark. As always, he shared the gospel message—this time on Cyprus, the island where he'd grown up.

Saul/Paul: This apostle was from Tarsus. As a Jew, he was probably often called by his Hebrew name, "Saul." He spoke both Hebrew and Greek. He was taught by a famous teacher named Gamaliel and became a Pharisee. He was very strict in following all the Jewish laws that Pharisees felt were important to obey. He also was a strong persecutor of Jesus' followers. But one day, when he was on the road to Damascus to bring back followers and put them in prison, he had a vision of Jesus Christ speaking to him. He became blind, and Ananias, a follower living in Damascus, healed him. After this, he changed completely and had a new purpose in life. Instead of *persecuting* Jesus' followers, he *became* a follower—and a leader. Filled with the Holy Spirit—or spiritual power—Paul traveled with various companions by land and sea to many places in the Roman Empire, sharing the message of the Christ, gaining new followers, forming new churches, and healing many people. Saul was also a Roman citizen. He began to use his Roman name, "Paul," perhaps because most of the people he taught were not Jews. He was known as the "apostle to the Gentiles." He was often opposed by those who were either jealous that others were listening to and following him or by those who did not believe his message. At various times he was persecuted—beaten, stoned, or put in prison. But with love and joy and faith he continued preaching the good news about Jesus' life and teachings. Paul healed many people through spiritual power alone—just as Jesus had. The Bible tells about some of these healings—of lameness, mental illness, serious physical injuries, snakebite, and stomach disease. Paul also restored a young boy to life after a fall from a third-floor window. Paul's life story, as told by Luke in Acts, and his words, as written in his letters to the churches, show how unselfishly and energetically Paul listened to and obeyed the Holy Spirit.

Jesus' Followers and Their Healing Mission

Several other followers of Jesus had the opportunity to travel with Paul and to support his preaching and healing ministry. Paul knew that they, too, were filled with spiritual power—the Holy Spirit. Some of these mentioned in the Bible are:

Silas: Paul chose Silas, or Silvanus, to travel with him to Macedonia. There in the city of Philippi, both men were imprisoned. As they prayed and sang hymns, an earthquake occurred, the prison doors opened, and they were free. Silas helped Paul as he preached and healed in several cities in Macedonia and Achaia, including Corinth. When Paul left this city, Silas remained. Paul spoke about him in his letters, telling of the good work he was doing.

Luke: Luke, or Lucas, is traditionally thought to be the writer of the book of Acts as well as the Gospel of Luke. Paul called him a "fellow worker." Luke first joined Paul in Troas in Asia and traveled with him much of the rest of Paul's life, accompanying him even to Rome.

Timothy: Timothy, or Timotheus, was from Derbe or Lystra. Paul loved him like a son. At times Timothy traveled with Paul, and at other times Paul sent him to places, such as Thessalonica, to teach and help the followers there. Later, Paul put him in charge of the church in Ephesus.

John Mark: John Mark, or Marcus, traveled with Paul and Barnabas for a short time on their first missionary journey. John Mark left them during the trip. Barnabas wanted to take him on his next journey with Paul, but Paul refused. This disagreement caused Paul and Barnabas to separate. Barnabas took John Mark with him to Cyprus. Later, Paul spoke kindly of John Mark.

Aristarchus: This follower was from Thessalonica. Among his trips with Paul was his journey to Rome when Paul was taken there as a prisoner. Aristarchus was a close and valued friend, staying with Paul, probably for as long as Paul lived.

Peter and John Heal Man of Lameness

Acts 3:1-11

Disciple/Apostle: In Acts, the word "disciple" means "student" and sometimes refers to one of Jesus' twelve closest students: Peter (Simon, Cephas); John; Andrew; James; James, son of Alphaeus; Thaddeus (Lebbaeus, Judas); Philip; Bartholomew (Nathaniel); Matthew (Levi); Thomas (Didymus); Simon the Canaanite (The Zealot); Judas Iscariot—and later, Matthias, chosen to replace Judas Iscariot. More often, "disciple" refers to a new follower of Jesus. "Apostle" means "one sent out." The twelve disciples and others who went out to heal and to teach and preach the good news about Jesus were called "apostles."

Peter and **John:** See page 6.

See Matthew 10:1-8; Mark 6:7-13; Luke 10:1-9,17-19.

Holy Spirit: See page 4.

In most cases the King James Version uses the term "Holy Ghost" for "Holy Spirit."

See Acts 1:8.

Jesus was the greatest spiritual healer in the world. He had many **disciples,** or students, but he chose twelve to be his closest disciples. **Peter** and **John** were two of these. Jesus sent them, as well as many others, to cities and towns to share the good news about God's love and power and to heal people. When the disciples were sent out, they were known as "**apostles.**" ▪

Jesus had promised his apostles that they would not be alone after he left them. He told them they would be filled with the **Holy Spirit.** ▪ ▪ This meant they would understand the truth that God is Spirit and His children are always spiritual, perfect, healthy, and loving. With this powerful spiritual understanding, they could go into the whole world and heal as Jesus had asked them to do.

Not long after Jesus was gone, many of his followers, including the twelve apostles,  were together in **Jerusalem.** It was the day of the religious festival called **Pentecost.** Suddenly, they were filled with the Holy Spirit. What Jesus had taught about God's great love was now very clear to them. The followers told a large crowd that day about the power of God. They told them in such a way that each one there could understand.

Then, Peter stood with the other eleven apostles to speak. The Jews were expecting the **Messiah,** or **Christ,** to come some day to help and heal. Peter told them that Jesus was the Christ. He spoke of Jesus' wonderful healings and that he had risen from the dead. He also said Jesus had been filled with the Holy Spirit. He explained that this spiritual power and understanding had filled the apostles that very day, and now everyone could receive this same power. That day, 3,000 people believed Peter and became Jesus' followers!

Judas was one of Jesus' twelve closest disciples, but he betrayed him. After Jesus was gone, his followers chose Matthias to replace Judas (Acts 1:13-15, 23-26).

Jerusalem: This is the most important city in the Bible. For centuries, Jews traveled to Jerusalem to worship God at special festivals held in the Temple (see **Temple** on page 12).

Pentecost: The word "Pentecost" in Greek means "fiftieth day." The Jews praised God for their grain harvest with a special Pentecost festival the day after the seven-week harvest (the fiftieth day). Christians see it as the day Jesus' followers were first filled with the Holy Spirit (Acts 2:1-41). The Bible tells us that the Pentecost experience—being filled with the Holy Spirit—occurred for all who became Jesus' followers from that time on.

Messiah/Christ: See page 3.

Peter also told the people to "repent" and be "baptized." One meaning of "repent" is to turn from wrong thinking and turn to God. Peter was telling the Jews that they could have a new life by following Jesus, whose life and teachings had shown that God is unlimited Love. (See **Baptism** on page 26.)

See Acts 2:14-41.

Temple: The Temple in Jerusalem was the center of the Jews' religious worship. More than just a place of prayer and public worship, the Temple symbolized the presence of God. Almost 1,000 years before Jesus, King David planned the Temple, and his son Solomon built it when he became king. It was very large and beautiful and built by skilled workers using the finest wood, stone, silver, and gold. The Temple contained a room called the "Holy of Holies," where the ark was kept. The ark was a chest that contained Moses' Ten Commandments on stone tablets, as well as other articles. The ark had disappeared by Jesus' time. This Temple was destroyed by an enemy in 586 B.C., rebuilt and finished in 515 B.C., and then destroyed again. King Herod the Great began to rebuild the Temple in 20 B.C. It was finished in 64 A.D.

The term "alms" is used in the King James Version and means something given to help the poor. The Jews believed that it was right to give to the needy. Since many people entered and left the Temple through this gate, it was a good place to beg for money. Jewish laws said that people who were sick or disabled were "unclean" or "impure" and could not enter the Temple area. Other Jews could not touch the sick or disabled or be touched by them because they would be considered "unclean," too.

Once after Pentecost, Peter and John were walking to the **Temple.** It was three o'clock in the afternoon. This was one of three times during the day when Jews in Jerusalem went to the Temple to pray. A man was there who had never been able to walk. Each day people carried him to the Temple gate called "Beautiful" so that he could beg for money. ◼ When he saw Peter and John going into the Temple, he asked them to give him something.

Peter and John looked right into the man's eyes. Peter said to him firmly, "Look at us." Peter wanted this man to pay attention to them. The man obeyed Peter and looked up at them—expecting to receive something.

Jesus had taught Peter and John well. He had shown them how important it is to see people the way God made them—as His children, happy, healthy, and strong, always the image and likeness of their Father-Mother God. So Peter and John thought only about God and His goodness when they saw this man.

Peter said to him, "I don't have money, but I will give you what I do have. In the **name of Jesus Christ** of Nazareth, rise up and walk." Peter wanted this man to know that he was being healed by the same understanding of God's power and goodness that Jesus had shown them in his healings.

Then Peter **took the man by the right hand** and lifted him up. Right away, the man's feet and ankle bones were strong and firm. Peter's words and actions showed his strong faith that the man was God's spiritual child and that God gave him the power to walk. This faith helped the man trust that he could walk.

Name of Jesus Christ: In the Bible a name represents the nature or character of someone. When Jesus' followers said they were doing something in the "name of Jesus Christ" they meant that they had faith that the same power and authority to heal that God gave Jesus was also given to them.

Laying On of Hands/Healing by Touch: In Bible times many people believed they could be healed by being touched by or by touching a holy man—someone close to God.

■ *Being touched ("laying on of hands"):* The term "laying on of hands" symbolized the power of God to heal. Jesus and his followers knew that human hands had no power to heal. Instead, placing hands on someone was an expression of love that helped remove fear. In half of Jesus' thirty recorded healings, no mention of touch is made. In fact, many times when Jesus touched people, he made it clear that it was faith that healed. Of the recorded healings of Jesus' followers, only half mention that people were touched in some way. Of those, two were just helped to their feet.

■ *Touching the holy person or his clothing:* Many people believed that if they touched a holy person, his shadow, or his clothing, they would be healed. Jesus and apostles like Peter and Paul were so spiritually minded that they were able to know people's need for healing. Those who reached out were healed because of Jesus' and the apostles' clear understanding of the all-power of God, who is Spirit, to heal.

WHAT CAN YOU DO?

What if you're not feeling well and can't seem to do the things you usually do? Remember the lame man at the Temple gate who had never walked. When Peter told him to get up and walk, the man obeyed. Peter and John learned from Jesus that God made everyone in His image and likeness, spiritual and perfect. They knew that if something was not spiritual and perfect, God didn't make it, and so it had no power. Peter and John knew it, and you can know it, too. You can take a stand for what is good and true, and you'll feel like your true self again.

The man jumped up, stood, and started to walk. As he went into the Temple with Peter and John, he was walking, leaping, and shouting out his thanks to God.

Everyone around them saw this man walking and jumping. They knew he was the beggar at the Beautiful Gate who had never walked. They were so amazed! They wondered how this had happened.

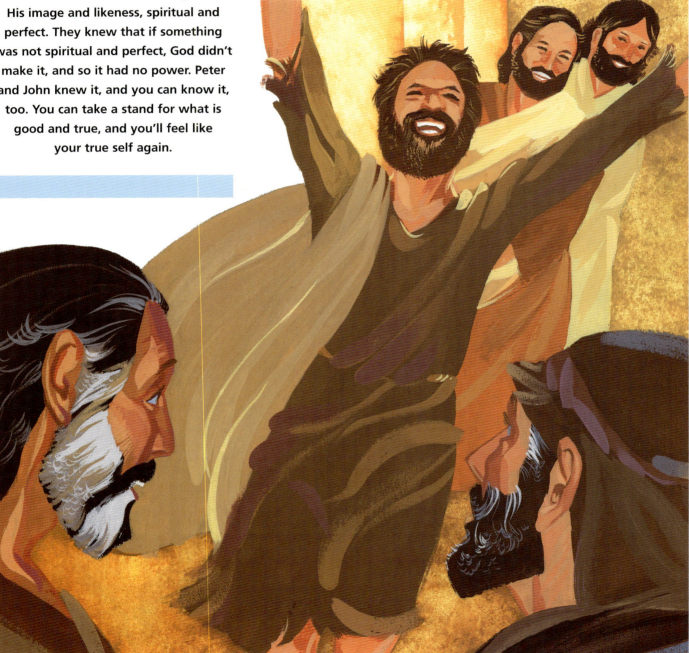

The man was so full of joy that he grabbed Peter and John and wouldn't let go. As the three reached the place in the Temple called **Solomon's Porch**, all the people there ran to see this wonderful healing for themselves.

Think what this meant to the man who had never walked! ■ And think what it meant to those who saw this happen. People must have been so happy to know that those who understood Jesus' teachings could heal, too!

Solomon's Porch: This was one of the covered walkways lined with marble columns that surrounded the Temple area. It was built by King Herod in the same area as the original porch built by King Solomon. Jesus taught there and so did the apostles.

Now that the man was healed and considered "clean" and "pure," the Jewish laws allowed him to go into the Temple and be in the company of his Jewish family and friends.

He that believeth on me, the works that I do shall he do also; and greater works than these shall he do.

John 14:12

Jesus was a great teacher who showed his disciples how to heal and how to pray with complete faith in God's goodness and love. They learned to trust that God, who created everyone spiritual and perfect, never gives them anything but good. We, too, can have faith that God always cares for us and the world. This will result in wonderful healings—just as it did for Jesus' disciples.

Stephen Heals Many People

Acts 6:8

Disciple/Apostle: See page 10.

Holy Spirit: See page 4.

See Acts 1:8.

Pentecost: See page 11.

Messiah/Christ: See page 3.

Here the Bible uses the term "disciples" to refer to Jesus' followers (Acts 6:1).

Here the Bible uses the term "brethren" to refer to Jesus' followers (Acts 6:3).

Stephen: See page 7.

See Acts 6:1-6.

While Jesus was still with his **apostles,** he told them that soon they would be filled with the **Holy Spirit,** which means they would be filled with spiritual thoughts about God and His power. ■

Just as Jesus had said, the apostles *did* receive the Holy Spirit. It was on the day of **Pentecost.** Right away, they were eager to share their new understanding and to encourage others to have faith in the teachings of Jesus **Christ.**

The number of Jesus' followers ■ grew. There were so many that the twelve apostles, Jesus' closest disciples, couldn't do all that was needed to take care of everyone. So they asked the followers ■ to choose seven men to help them. These men needed to be good and wise and filled with spiritual understanding and power. One of the men chosen was **Stephen.** ■ But Stephen did more than help the apostles in this way.

Stephen also healed. He had great faith in God and in Jesus' teachings. Stephen knew, as Jesus did, that God created His children in His likeness—spiritual and perfect—and is always giving them only good. Because of Stephen's great faith, he was able to heal many people.

Stephen was also a good speaker. He listened to God's good ideas so he would know just what to say to others. He helped many people know more about God's power and goodness and about Jesus' life and teachings. Because of this, many more people became Jesus' followers.

Think how happy the early followers were to have this great healer and speaker with them!

Some of the Jews accused Stephen of speaking against Moses. Stephen defended himself before the Jewish council. He said that in the past, Jewish leaders had resisted the idea that God is Spirit. They had worshiped God in a material place—the Temple—with rituals (see **Temple,** page 12). When Jesus, their Messiah, came, he gave them a more spiritual way to worship, but they killed him. After Stephen spoke, the Jewish leaders were so angry that they killed him, too (Acts 6:9-15; Acts 7:1-60).

The words that I speak unto you, they are spirit, and they are life.

John 6:63

What powerful words Jesus spoke to his followers! He taught spiritual truths about God's great love and care for all His children. These truths healed. Followers like Stephen knew that God's love was all-powerful, and they were able to heal as Jesus did. We can do this, too!

?

WHAT CAN YOU DO?

If you think what you do isn't important, remember Stephen. He was given a simple job and did it gladly, but he didn't stop there. Understanding the power of God's love, Stephen also healed and shared the good news. You can listen for God's special ways to help others, too.

Philip Heals People of Illnesses, Paralysis, and Lameness

Acts 8:5-8

Disciple/Apostle: See page 10.

Holy Spirit: See page 4.

See Acts 1:8.

Pentecost: See page 11.

Philip: See page 7.

Jerusalem: See page 11.

See Acts 6:1-6; Acts 8:1-4.

Jesus gave one last message to his **apostles** when he was still with them. He told them that soon they would be filled with the **Holy Spirit.** This meant that their thoughts would be filled with the spirit and energy of God's goodness and power. This spirit would be with them forever so that they could heal others and take the message of God's love to the world. ■ When Jesus' followers were gathered together on the day of **Pentecost,** they *were* filled with the Holy Spirit—just as Jesus had said.

The followers shared this new understanding with others, and many people became Jesus' followers. The twelve apostles, those closest to Jesus, needed help taking care of all these people, so they chose seven men for this job—men who were wise and filled with the Holy Spirit. **Philip** was one of those chosen. Soon after this, the Jewish leaders in **Jerusalem** began to treat Jesus' followers very badly. This made many of the followers, including Philip, leave the city quickly. ■

The Samaritans' ancestors were Jews who had married people who were not Jews. For this and other reasons, the Jews refused to allow the Samaritans to help rebuild the Temple in Jerusalem. (See **Temple** on page 12 and **Jerusalem** on page 11.) The Samaritans built their own temple in Gerizim. Jesus encouraged his followers to treat Samaritans the way they would want to be treated themselves—with kindness and love (Luke 9:52-56; Luke 10: 30-37; Luke 17:11-19; John 4:3-42).

Messiah/Christ: See page 3.

Philip's ministry into Samaria helped Jesus' followers see that their mission was for the whole world and not just for the Jews.

WHAT CAN YOU DO?

Sometimes the bad things others do can seem to take away your happiness and peace or try to stop you from doing good. When some people treated Jesus' followers badly, Philip listened to God's direction and went to new places where he could keep helping others. Like Philip, you can pray and listen to what God is telling you to do. You can know that evil has no power to stop good because God is the only power. When you listen to God's good thoughts, you'll see that nothing can steal your happiness or stop you from doing good.

Philip went to a city in Samaria and taught the people there. Most Jews didn't even travel through this region. For many years the Jews and Samaritans had not been friends. They had argued that they each had the best place to worship God. ■ Jesus had visited a city there and talked to many Samaritans. He had spoken about God who is Spirit. He had helped them understand that the best way for everyone to worship God was spiritually—in thought. The place didn't matter. The Samaritans had listened to what he said and believed that he was the **Messiah,** or **Christ.**

Jesus had told his followers that after he was gone, they should go to Samaria, as well as other places, to teach about him. Philip was one of the first followers to go to Samaria. ■

Trust in the Lord with all thine heart; and lean not unto thine own understanding.

Proverbs 3:5

Philip was filled with the spiritual understanding of God's goodness and power. He didn't let wrong thoughts crowd out his trust in God.
We, too, have spiritual understanding right at hand to help us in trouble of any kind. We can have faith that God created us perfect and keeps us this way. We can know that there is no other power or understanding that can make us afraid. Trusting God with all our heart brings healing.

The people who heard Philip teach paid attention to what he said because he healed many people who were ill, **paralyzed,** or lame. Philip was filled with the Holy Spirit—with spiritual thoughts about God's love and power. He knew that God, who is Spirit, creates everyone in His image and likeness, spiritual and perfect. Philip was sure that God gives only good to His children. He was able to heal because of this faith in God's goodness and care.

The Samaritans were so happy that Philip was with them. They were very grateful to see all these wonderful healings!

Ananias Heals Saul of Blindness

Acts 9:1-19

Other accounts of this story are found in Acts 22:3-16 and Acts 26:4-18.

Saul/Paul: See page 8.

Jerusalem: See page 11.

Messiah/Christ: See page 3.

See Acts 8:3.

Damascus: This was an important city in Syria. It was about a six-day trip from Jerusalem.

The high priest was the head of the Sanhedrin, the council of Jewish leaders.

Synagogue: The place where Jews met to worship God on the Sabbath day, which was Saturday.

Here, the Bible calls Jesus' followers "any of this way." Jesus called himself "the way, the truth, and the life" (John 14:6).

Saul was a Jew in **Jerusalem** who was not happy that every day more and more people were becoming followers of **Christ** Jesus. He decided to do something about it—he went to their homes and dragged both men and women outside and took them to prison.

Saul knew that many followers had escaped to **Damascus,** so he decided to go after them. He asked the high priest of the Jewish council for letters he could take to the Damascus **synagogues** where the followers were preaching about Jesus. These letters would tell the synagogue leaders that he had the right to bring the followers back to Jerusalem to put them in prison. But something happened on his way to Damascus…

Two other accounts of this story say that it was noon when Saul and those traveling with him saw this light. It was much brighter than the sun (Acts 22:6; Acts 26:13).

Lord: After Jesus' resurrection, his followers sometimes used this term for him because they deeply respected his Godlikeness. They were seeing him as the "Master," who had power over death. Jesus expressed the highest possible spiritual understanding of God. He was the "Way-shower," helping his followers gain a better understanding of God who is Love. He also showed them their relationship to God as His spiritual children—His image and likeness, reflecting spiritual power over sin, sickness, and death.

Here in Acts 9:6 the King James Version adds, "Lord, what wilt thou have me to do?" (This is also found in most translations in Acts 22:10.)

Here in Acts 9:5, the King James Version adds that Jesus told Saul: "It is hard for thee to kick against the pricks." (This sentence is also found in most translations in Acts 26:14.) A "prick" was a sharpened stick that farmers used for guiding farm animals in the right direction. Jesus was saying that just as a farm animal might resist following a farmer's direction, Saul had resisted obeying God's direction, and it was painful for him.

Saul was almost to the city when suddenly a very bright light shined all around him. ■ He called this a light from "heaven," showing that he felt God was present with him. When he saw this light, he fell to the ground. Then, he heard a voice saying to him, "Saul, Saul, why do you do these terrible things to me?"

Saul shook with fear and was amazed. He replied, "Who are you, **Lord**?" ■

And the Lord said, "I am Jesus, and you are doing terrible things to me." ■

Jesus then said, "Get up and go into the city. There, you will be told what you must do." ■

The men traveling with Saul stood still and didn't say a word. They had heard the voice, but they didn't see anyone talking. ■

Saul got up and found that even with his eyes open, he couldn't see at all. The people with him had to lead him by the hand and take him into Damascus.

He spent three days there without being able to see. During that time he didn't eat or drink. ■

Here, another account of this story tells that Jesus gave special instructions to Saul about taking the message of Jesus Christ to others (Acts 26:16-18).

The other two accounts of this story give slightly different details (Acts 22:9; Acts 26:13,14).

Perhaps Saul didn't eat or drink because he was confused about all that had just happened. He was upset and probably didn't even think about food. But also, Saul was a faithful Jew. Jews sometimes fasted (didn't eat) to express humility and devotion to God and sadness or guilt for doing wrong.

Ananias: See page 7.

See Acts 22:12.

The Bible says that Saul had a vision of Ananias "putting his hand on him, that he might receive his sight." Putting hands on someone symbolized the power of God to heal. (See **Laying On of Hands/Healing by Touch** on page 13.)

A disciple of Jesus named **Ananias** lived in Damascus. Ananias was a faithful Jew who obeyed the Jewish laws. Other Jews liked and respected him. ▪ Ananias heard Jesus speak to him in a vision and say, "Ananias!"

Ananias answered, "Yes, Lord, I am here."

Then Ananias heard Jesus say, "Get up and go to Straight Street. Find Judas' house and ask for a man from Tarsus named Saul. At this very moment, Saul is praying. He has seen in a vision a man named Ananias coming into the house and healing him of his blindness." ▪

But Ananias didn't really want to go to Saul.

He answered, "Lord, many people have told me about this man Saul and the terrible things he did to your followers  in Jerusalem. Now, he's here in Damascus—and he has permission from the chief priests to make your followers prisoners and take them back to Jerusalem to be punished."

But Jesus said to Ananias, "Go to Saul. I have chosen him ▮ to take my message to the **Gentiles** and to kings, as well as to the Jews. ▮ I will explain to him that taking the good news to others will not be an easy thing to do." Jesus knew that not everyone would understand the message or accept it. Saul would have to be very strong in his faith in God because at times people would not be kind to him.

Ananias listened and obeyed.

Here the Bible uses the term "saints," which means those who are "Godlike" or "pure."

The King James Version says that Jesus describes Saul as a "chosen vessel." In Greek the word "vessel" can mean anything that is useful or helpful. Saul was to be a great help to Jesus as his apostle. He would go into the world and teach people about Jesus and heal as he had done (Acts 9:15).

Gentiles: This is the term Jews used for people who were not Jews. Most Gentiles did not worship the one God.

Here the King James Version calls the Jews "children of Israel." This is because Jews were "children" or descendants of the twelve sons of Jacob, who was also called "Israel." Jacob was one of the Jews' most honored ancestors (Acts 9:15).

By using the term "brother," Ananias was welcoming Saul into fellowship with all of Jesus' followers.

Holy Spirit: See page 4.

Here, the Bible says that it was as if scales, or flakes, had fallen from Saul's eyes (Acts 9:18).

Baptism: Jesus taught that baptism was the act of being filled with the Holy Spirit—spiritual understanding and power (Acts 1:5). After his resurrection, Jesus promised his followers that they would be baptized, or filled, with the Holy Spirit. And on the day of Pentecost that is just what happened. In the early Christian church, Jesus' followers baptized (dipped, poured or washed) with water. This ritual symbolized that the people being baptized believed Jesus was the Christ and that they wanted to be his followers. (See **Messiah/Christ** on page 3.) It also symbolized the purification of thought. This was what Paul called "putting off the old man" (getting rid of the belief that people are material) and "putting on the new man" (lifting thought to see everyone's spiritual selfhood created by God) (Colossians 3:9,10). With this spiritual understanding, Jesus and his followers were able to heal sickness and sin and to overcome death.

Ananias went to the house where Saul was staying. He entered, touched Saul, and said to him, "Brother ▮ Saul, Jesus, whom you saw in a vision as you were coming here, talked with me, too. He sent me to you so that you could see again and be filled with the **Holy Spirit.**" Immediately, Saul was able to see, ▮ and he got up. He was filled with a new understanding of God's goodness and power, and he was healed.

Ananias knew that nothing is impossible to God. Jesus had proved the power of God to his followers by healing. He had given them an understanding of God's love for all His creation. Ananias knew how important it was to forgive Saul—because love can heal anyone.

Next, Saul was **baptized.** Sometimes people were baptized by being washed in water. This showed that they had become Jesus' followers. Baptism was also a way for people to say that they had gotten rid of wrong thoughts and had turned to Godlike thoughts.

Saul felt the power of the Holy Spirit—the Spirit of truth. He had not eaten for three days, but now he was ready to have a meal. Ananias and Judas, the owner of the house, and some other followers, too, may have eaten with him. By doing this, they would have been showing Saul that they forgave and trusted him. Their forgiveness would have made Saul's faith in Jesus' life and teachings even stronger. After this, Saul stayed with Jesus' followers in Damascus for several days.

What a wonderful spiritual healing this had been for Saul! He had gone to Damascus to do terrible things to Jesus' followers and, instead, he was healed by one of those followers. Not only could he see with his eyes, but he could also see, or understand, the truth about Jesus. Saul became one of Jesus' best followers and learned to teach and heal as he did.

Ye have heard that it hath been said, Thou shalt love thy neighbour, and hate thine enemy. But I say unto you, Love your enemies, bless them that curse you, do good to them that hate you, and pray for them which despitefully use you, and persecute you.

Matthew 5:43, 44

When someone hates us, it can be hard not to hate that person back. But Jesus taught us to love our enemies, and he taught us how. We can see those who hate us as God sees them—as His children, lovable, pure, and perfect. Loving like this is a prayer that changes thought. And when our thought changes, good things happen in our lives.

?

WHAT CAN YOU DO?

If people are unkind to you, it may be hard to forgive them. But you can remember Ananias and how he forgave Saul. You can know, as Ananias did, that God, who is Love, cares for all His children. You can know that anyone who is unkind is really God's child—perfect and loving always. So bad actions aren't ever part of anyone's real self. This spirit of love that God gives you wipes away all hurt or hate. It frees you to act kindly and share the love that's always in your heart.

Peter Heals Aeneas of Paralysis

Acts 9:32-35

Pentecost: See page 11.

Disciple/Apostle: See page 10.

Holy Spirit: See page 4.

Jerusalem: See page 11.

See Acts 2:43.

Bed: In Bible times some beds were of wood. Others were simple floor mats, perhaps of straw.

Peter: See page 6 .

See Acts 5:12-16.

On the day of **Pentecost,** Jesus' **apostles** and other followers were filled with the **Holy Spirit.** They knew that God is spirit, the only power, and that He is always present to heal. After that, the apostles healed many people in **Jerusalem** through the power of God. And large crowds of both men and women became followers. After Peter healed a man who had never walked, people brought the sick into the streets on their **beds** so that if **Peter** passed by, he would heal them. Many from outside Jerusalem also brought those who were sick—and they were all healed!

Palestine: See page 10.

Church: The Greek word for "church" means "gathering." Early Christians had no church buildings. Therefore, a "church" was a group of followers. Groups met either outdoors or in someone's home.

See Acts 9:31.

Here, the Bible uses the word "saints," which means those who are "Godlike" or "pure."

Paralysis: See page 20.

Jesus' healing: Matthew 9:1-8; Mark 2:1-12; Luke 5:17-26. Peter's healing: See "Peter and John Heal Man of Lameness" on page 10.

All over **Palestine,** the followers began meeting in groups. They called their groups "**churches**." The followers had a deep love for Jesus and his teachings. They were filled with the spiritual understanding and power of God—and this comforted and encouraged them. The churches continued to have new people joining them. ▪

Peter traveled around the country visiting the churches and talking with the followers. ▪ He brought the good news about Jesus and what he had taught of God's powerful love and goodness.

One of the towns Peter visited in his travels was Lydda. There, he found a man named Aeneas, who was **paralyzed.** For eight years, Aeneas had stayed in bed because he hadn't been able to walk. When Peter saw Aeneas, he knew that he could help him. Peter had learned about healing from listening to Jesus teach and from watching him heal. He had seen Jesus heal a man who was paralyzed. And Peter himself had healed a man in Jerusalem who had never walked. ▪

Messiah/Christ: See page 3.

Here the King James Version says "Saron." This refers to the "Plain of Sharon," which is the large area between Joppa and Caesarea.

He giveth power to the faint; and to them that have no might he increaseth strength.

Isaiah 40:29

Peter knew that God who is Love is powerful and active, and tenderly cares for everyone. Peter knew that Love would strengthen and heal the man who couldn't walk. And he was right! We, too, can know and feel this Love right here and now, giving care and strength to us—and everyone.

WHAT CAN YOU DO?

You may know someone who has a handicap—maybe he or she can't walk very well or hear or talk clearly. Like Peter, you can fill your thoughts with God's tender care for that person. Your good thoughts are a prayer that can help bring happiness and healing.

Peter spoke to Aeneas with great faith and strength. He said, "Aeneas, Jesus **Christ** heals you!" Peter was telling Aeneas that the healing power was the Christ, the spiritual nature that Jesus expressed. Jesus knew that God, who is Spirit, made His children in His likeness. This likeness is spiritual and perfect, healthy and strong. Peter knew that this Christ-like thinking was his own thinking, too—and it was healing Aeneas.

Next, Peter commanded him, "Get up and make your bed!" Peter was humbly trusting God's love for this man. He wanted Aeneas to see that he was completely well and didn't need to stay in bed. Instantly, Aeneas stood up. He was healed!

When the people who lived in Lydda and the whole area ■ saw Aeneas walking, they all became Jesus' followers!

Peter Restores Tabitha to Life

Acts 9:36-42

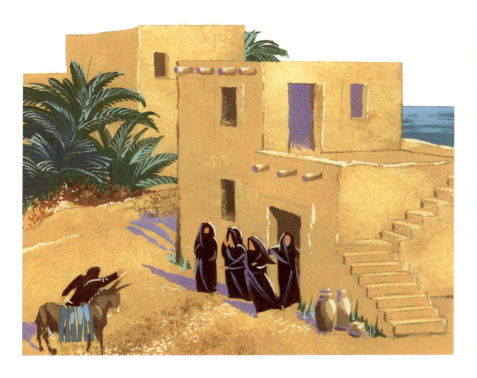

Messiah/Christ: See page 3.

Tabitha: The King James Version says this woman was a "disciple," meaning "student," and that she was full of "almsdeeds." This means she was always caring for poor and needy people, giving gifts, and helping them. She did many "good works," or acts of love and kindness. She was someone the other followers loved and respected greatly. Her Hebrew name, "Tabitha," is the same as the Greek name "Dorcas." Both words mean "gazelle," which is a small deer. Luke, the writer of Acts, may have given the Greek translation of her name to show that she expressed grace and gentleness—like a gazelle.

Burial Customs: Preparation for burial would have included washing the body and then wrapping it in linen with oils and spices. Jews usually buried people on the day they died.

Upper Room: Sometimes people built a room on the roof that could be used for various activities. There, people might visit with guests, hold feasts, or pray. The breezes made it a cool place to sleep in the summer.

Some followers of Jesus **Christ** lived in the city of Joppa, which was by the Mediterranean Sea. One of the followers, **Tabitha,** loved people and did many good and kind things for those who needed help. She must have brought happiness to everyone around her.

But Tabitha became sick and died. The followers in Joppa must have prayed the way they knew Jesus prayed when someone died. Jesus knew that God was everyone's life. He knew that life was more powerful than death. And he had proved this when he rose from the dead. The followers' prayers would have given them hope that their friend would come back to life through the power of God. So instead of **getting her ready to be buried,** they washed her and laid her in a **room upstairs.**

Then they heard some wonderful news.

Here the Bible calls the followers "disciples." (See **Disciple/Apostle** on page 10.)

Peter: See page 6.

Jerusalem: See page 11.

Temple: See page 12.

The Bible gives these examples of people Jesus restored to life:
- Widow's son (Luke 7:11-17)
- Jairus' daughter (Matthew 9:18,19,23-26; Mark 5:21-24, 35-43; Luke 8:40-42,49-56)
- Lazarus (John 11:1-44)
- Jesus himself (Matthew 28:1-10; Mark 16:1-8; Luke 24:1-12; John 20:1-18).

Examples of people Peter healed up to this time were:
- Lame man (See "Peter and John Heal Man of Lameness" on page 10.)
- Many people in the streets of Jerusalem (Acts 5:12-16)
- Aeneas (See "Peter Heals Aeneas of Paralysis" on page 28.)

The followers heard that the apostle **Peter** was in Lydda, just a half-day trip away. They had faith that Peter could bring Tabitha back to life, so they sent two men to get him. When they found Peter, they asked him to hurry back to Joppa. Right away he got up and went with the men.

Peter had healed many in **Jerusalem**—first, a man at the **Temple** who couldn't walk and then other sick people who were brought to him. And people in Lydda were talking about another man Peter had healed—a man right in their own city. He had been paralyzed. Peter had seen Jesus bring several people back to life. And Jesus' own resurrection from death showed Peter even more clearly that death could be overcome. Peter had seen these things with his own eyes. He knew that life was more powerful that death, and he was ready to prove God's great power.

When Peter came to the house, they took him to the upstairs room. In this room were many women whose husbands had died. They were called "widows." Tabitha had been a great help to them, and they were very sad about her death. They may have been worried about what they would do without her. When Peter arrived, they went over and stood beside him, **crying loudly** and showing him the clothes Tabitha had made.

Peter must have remembered something Jesus had done once when he brought someone back to life. People had been crying loudly there, too—and Jesus had told them all to leave. He didn't want people to be there who didn't have faith in the power of God to bring someone back to life. He wanted only good thoughts—thoughts of life—to be there. Peter knew he needed to do what Jesus had done, so he sent all the crying women out of the room. Then, he was alone with powerful thoughts of God's love for Tabitha. Peter was knowing with all his heart that life—not death—was the only power.

Jewish Mourning Customs: In Bible times when someone died, people visited the person's family to show their love and to help them. The usual mourning period for family members was seven days. The Jews also followed certain rituals to show their grief. Those in mourning wore clothes made of sackcloth—a rough, dark-colored material made of goat's or camel's hair. Often, they "rent," or tore, their clothes. Some put ashes or dust on their heads.

See these verses in the story of Jairus' daughter: Matthew 9:24, 25; Mark 5:40; Luke 8:51-54.

?

WHAT CAN YOU DO?

What can you do when you need help right away? You can remember what the followers in Joppa did when their friend Tabitha died. They weren't afraid. They knew God would give them an answer. Very soon after Tabitha's death, they got the answer. They heard that Peter was nearby, and that he had a great understanding of God's power to heal. They wanted Peter to come and be with them and pray for Tabitha. So they sent for him. When you need help, you can listen for God's answer. His love and care are always with you to comfort you and to guide you to do the right thing.

Laying On of Hands/Healing by Touch: See page 13.

Here, the Bible uses the word "saints," which means those who are "Godlike" or "pure."

When thou prayest, enter into thy closet, and when thou hast shut thy door, pray to thy Father which is in secret; and thy Father which seeth in secret shall reward thee openly.

Matthew 6:6

Peter had learned from Jesus how to pray. He knew he needed to shut out all thoughts that were not about life and goodness. He needed to let his thinking be filled with messages from God. He knew that God who is Love fills all space and held Tabitha safe in His love. Peter listened quietly. And God answered his prayer as He always does, with happiness, peace, healing. We can pray as Peter prayed and trust as Peter trusted. Then, we will hear God's answers to our prayers, too.

Peter turned away from Tabitha and kneeled down to pray. He turned his thought away from death and turned it completely to God. He knew the power to bring Tabitha back to life came from God—not from him. He knew and felt the great power of God's love right there. He knew it was stronger than death.

Peter then turned to the woman and said, "Tabitha, get up." And she opened her eyes. When she saw Peter, she sat up. Then, **he took her by the hand** and helped her get up from her bed. It was a very special time— Peter had proved that life can never end.

Peter must have been eager to call the followers ▪ and widows who were waiting downstairs. He showed them that Tabitha was alive and well. Think what this meant to everyone! It strengthened their faith in God's power and care for all. News of this healing spread all over the city of Joppa. Many more people believed in the power of God to heal, and they became followers of Jesus, too!

Barnabas Heals Many People

Acts 14:1-3

Another account of Barnabas' healing work is found in Acts 15:12.

Barnabas: See page 8.

Holy Spirit: See page 4.

Saul/Paul: See page 8.

Messiah/Christ: See page 3.

See "Ananias Heals Saul of Blindness" on page 21.

See Acts 9:26-28.

Paul's Names: As a Jew and a Roman citizen, Paul had both a Hebrew and a Roman name (see Acts 13:9).

Church: See page 29.

See Acts 13:1-52.

Barnabas was a man who had great faith in God. He was filled with the **Holy Spirit**—with the truth that God is always present and all-powerful. He was a gentle man, and others liked him very much. Once he was kind to a man named **Saul** when other followers of **Christ** Jesus were afraid of him. Some time before this, Saul had tried to get rid of the followers. Barnabas told them that Saul had changed and that he was now a follower of Jesus, too. He showed them that they could trust Saul just as he did. A few years after this, Barnabas traveled with Saul, who was also called by his **Roman name Paul.** They went to many places to teach, to heal, and to start **churches.**

Gentiles: See page 25.

Be strong and of a good courage; be not afraid, neither be thou dismayed: for the Lord thy God is with thee whithersoever thou goest.

Joshua 1:9

If others are unkind to us, we can be unafraid, knowing that God who is Love is always with us. Barnabas and Paul were not afraid—even when people were saying terrible things about them. They were so filled with the goodness and power of God that they were very calm. They just kept praying and teaching and healing. God helped them do what they needed to do, and He will help us, too!

WHAT CAN YOU DO?

Have you ever seen others treat someone unkindly and you wanted to help? You might be afraid that if you do what is right, you might lose some friends. But you can let God's love fill your heart to overflowing. God is your Father-Mother, tenderly caring for all. You can know that God blesses you and you can be kind and loving. And no matter what anyone says, your good thoughts and prayers will help you and others, too. God's great love is with you and everyone—forever.

One of the cities Barnabas and Paul visited was Iconium. There, they spoke with great power and joy to both Jews and **Gentiles** about Jesus and his life. Many of these people became Jesus' followers. But some of the Jews were upset with Barnabas and Paul because they didn't like what they taught. They stirred up the Gentiles, who also became angry with the two men.

Even so, Barnabas and Paul did not stop their preaching. They stayed in Iconium for a long time and spoke boldly and without fear to the people. Barnabas, like Paul, was very spiritually minded. He knew that God, who is Spirit, created everyone in His likeness. He knew that God would never let His likeness be sick or in pain or disabled in any way. His thoughts were so filled with the Holy Spirit—the truth that God is the only power—that sickness was not even part of his thinking. And this spiritual knowing or prayer healed many people in Iconium. His friend Paul healed people there, too. The people who were healed must have been so grateful to learn about God's love and to see this love heal them.

Paul Heals Man of Lameness

Acts 14:8-10

Saul once tried to get rid of the followers of Jesus **Christ.** But after a wonderful healing, he was changed forever, and he became a follower, too. ▉ During the next few years, Saul spent time in several cities and regions. Sometimes he was in quiet thought and prayer, learning about Jesus' life and teachings. Sometimes he was talking to others about Jesus. Another follower, **Barnabas,** found him in his hometown of Tarsus and brought him to Antioch. ▉ Barnabas and Saul, who was also called by his **Roman name Paul,** then traveled together to many cities. There they taught, healed, and started **churches.** ▉

In the city of Iconium, Paul and Barnabas healed many people. These healings showed that what Jesus had taught about God's power to heal was true. And now Paul and Barnabas were teaching others about this power.

Saul/Paul: See page 8.

Messiah/Christ: See page 3.

See "Ananias Heals Saul of Blindness" on page 21.

Barnabas: See page 8.

It was in Antioch, Syria, that Jesus' followers were first called "Christians" (Acts 11:26).

Paul's Names: See page 35.

Church: See page 29.

Another follower, John Mark, joined Saul and Barnabas on the first part of their trip (Acts 12:25). See **John Mark** on page 9.

Opposition to Paul:
Paul's teaching and healing convinced many Jews to become followers of Jesus. This often made Jewish leaders jealous because they were losing power and authority over their followers.

After Paul's healing of blindness (see "Ananias Heals Saul of Blindness" on page 21) and before the healing of the lame man in this story, Paul visited many places. He taught and healed in many of these regions: Syria, Arabia, Palestine, Cilicia, Cyprus, Pamphylia, Pisidia, Lycaonia (see Acts 9:19-30; Galatians 1:15-17; Acts 11:22-30; Acts 12:24-14:3).

Individual healings in all these places aren't recorded in the Bible. But at the end of this trip, Paul traveled to Jerusalem. During his stay there, he told the apostles that he and Barnabas had healed Gentiles through the power of God in the many cities and regions they visited (Acts 15:12). (See **Gentiles** on page 25.) Healing was a natural result of Paul and Barnabas' faith in God's power and love for all. It's reasonable to think that people would learn of their healing power and would ask for help wherever they went.

Holy Spirit: See page 4.

See Acts 14:4-7.

But even after these wonderful healings, people in Iconium **turned the crowds against Paul** and Barnabas. The two had to leave because these people planned to kill them. They escaped to the city of Lystra. They didn't stop preaching because of what had happened. They were so filled with the **Holy Spirit**—with spiritual power—that they told everyone who would listen about Jesus.

In the crowd at Lystra was a man who really needed their help.

Gentiles: See page 25.

WHAT CAN YOU DO?

Sometimes a problem may seem so big that you feel you don't have the faith that will heal it. Think about Paul—even when he saw a man who had never walked, Paul was sure of God's power to heal. And that's what faith is all about—trusting God. You can have this strong faith, too. You can know that healing always comes from God. When you trust that the Almighty God is doing the work, you'll find your faith is powerful. The problem won't seem so big any more. In fact, when you know God is in control, you'll find you're healed.

This was a man who had never been able to walk. He was listening closely to what Paul had to say. Most of the people in Lystra were **Gentiles**—people who didn't believe in the one God, who is Spirit. But Paul could tell that this man had faith that he could be healed. When he looked at the man, he didn't pay attention to what was wrong with him. Instead, he knew that God is Spirit and that this man was God's child—perfect and spiritual. He knew with all his heart that this man *could* walk—that God made him able to walk and kept him that way. He looked the man straight in the eye and shouted, "Stand up!"

And the man did just that! In fact, he *jumped* up and started walking. Paul's complete faith in God's goodness and love for His children had healed the man.

How happy and thankful he must have been to walk for the very first time in his life!

Your faith should not stand in the wisdom of men, but in the power of God.

I Corinthians 2:5

Paul was a great spiritual healer. He had faith, not in his own power to heal but in the power Christ Jesus had shown—which is God's power. Even when a problem seemed hopeless—like not being able to walk—Paul stood fast in God's power. He knew, as Jesus knew, that God created His children in His image and likeness—spiritual and perfect—and always protects them from harm of every kind. We can know this, too, and heal just as Paul did. Our faith will then be "in the power of God."

Paul Heals Himself of Injuries

Acts 14:19, 20

Saul/Paul: See page 8.

Barnabas: See page 8.

The people of Lystra were very superstitious. When Paul healed the lame man, the people thought he and Barnabas were two of the gods they believed in. They thought Paul was Mercury (Hermes), the messenger of the gods, and Barnabas was Jupiter (Zeus), the king of the gods. They even brought oxen (with wreaths around their necks) to sacrifice to Paul and Barnabas (Acts 14:11-18).

Opposition to Paul: See page 38.

The Bible does not clearly state that Paul was dead but that those who stoned him "thought" he was dead. Stoning was a harsh method of killing someone. Heavy rocks were thrown at victims until no breath was left in them. So Paul certainly may have been dead. At the very least, he would have been so badly injured that there were no signs of life.

Paul was in Lystra, where he had healed a man who had never been able to walk. When this happened, the people were amazed. They believed in many gods, rather than the one God. They thought that Paul and his friend **Barnabas** were gods and began to worship them. Right away Paul told the people that there was only one God, who created everything. He talked about God's goodness and how God gives good to everyone. ■

The people finally stopped trying to worship Paul and Barnabas—but then something worse happened. The same Jews **who had turned the crowds against them** in other cities came to Lystra. They got the people there so upset with Paul that they wanted to kill him and began throwing heavy stones at him. When they were sure he was dead, ■ they dragged his body outside the town and left it there.

40

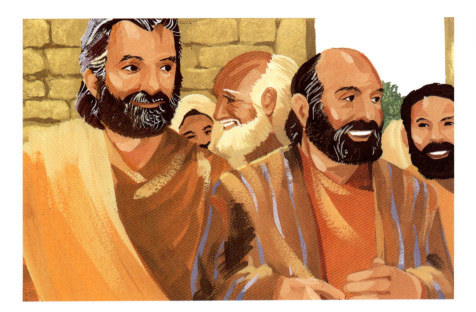

WHAT CAN YOU DO?

Are you afraid when you see others fighting or hurting each other? Remember Paul when a crowd of people stoned him. When he saw those men coming toward him, Paul knew that God was right there with him and that His goodness was more powerful than stones. Paul was absolutely sure that nothing could separate him from God's love. His prayer helped him to be brave and strong. Like Paul, you can know that no one can ever be separated from God's care. When you fill your thought with God's love and power, you'll be less afraid. God will keep you—and others—safe!

Even while the stones were being thrown at him, Paul would have been praying, knowing that his life was always in God's care—and that God's love always kept him safe. As he lay on the ground, some of Jesus' followers from Lystra gathered around him. They had just been learning from Paul about Jesus, who had risen from the dead. They showed their love, as well as their bravery, by trying to help Paul.

Just then, Paul got up! And he walked right back into Lystra without fear. What an awesome healing this was! Paul had been so badly hurt that people had thought he was dead, but now he got up and walked. His good thoughts, and those of Jesus' followers, were more powerful than those stones that had been thrown at him. What a wonderful proof of God's power this was. And how happy and thankful the followers must have been! The very next day Paul and Barnabas left for the city of Derbe—at least a day's trip away on foot or donkey. There, they continued teaching the good news about Jesus. And many more people became followers of Jesus!

The Spirit itself beareth witness with our spirit, that we are the children of God.

Romans 8:16

God, who is Spirit, creates us, gives us energy, keeps us alive. We are His children, made in His likeness—truly spiritual. If something happens to our human body, it can't touch our real spiritual life. Paul understood these truths. When angry men attacked him, he knew that nothing could take away his real spiritual life. This understanding quickly restored his strength and helped him go on his way. We too can know that our life and energy come from God who is Spirit. Spirit keeps us safe forever.

Paul Heals Young Girl of Mental Illness

Acts 16:16-18

Saul/Paul: See page 8.

Barnabas: See page 8.

Jerusalem: See page 11.

Church: See page 29.

Gentiles: See page 25.

After Paul was healed of his injuries (see "Paul Heals Himself of Injuries" on page 40) and before the healing in this story, he visited many regions, including: Palestine, Samaria, Phenicia (Phenice), Syria, Cilicia, Lycaonia, Galatia, Pisidia, Mysia, Pamphylia, Phrygia (Acts 14:21–16:15). Later, Paul wrote to the Christian churches in Galatia, strengthening their faith. He reminded them that the healings that were happening among them were through the Holy Spirit (Galatians 3:5). Everywhere Paul traveled, it was his mission to teach people about the power of the Spirit to help and to heal.

Silas: See page 9.

Messiah/Christ: See page 3.

After **Paul** was healed of his injuries from stoning, he and **Barnabas** went home to Antioch and **Jerusalem.** There, they told about the **churches** that were growing and the **Gentiles** who had been healed on their trip. Then, Paul and his new helper, **Silas,** left from Antioch and began a new trip. First, they went back to many cities Paul had visited before, encouraging the followers of **Christ** Jesus and teaching them more about him.

Then, they set out to new cities,  crossing the Aegean Sea to Macedonia. In the city of Philippi, they found a small group of Jewish women who met for prayer by a river. A woman named **Lydia** was with them. She loved Paul's teachings and became a follower of Jesus.

Two other followers joined Paul and Silas—Timothy at Lystra and Luke at Troas. (See **Timothy** and **Luke** on page 9.)

Lydia: Lydia was a businesswoman and was probably wealthy. She sold expensive purple cloth—a color loved by the rich. It's very possible that she was a Gentile who prayed with the Jewish women. She may have been the first person in Europe to become a follower of Jesus (Acts 16:13-15).

The Bible says the girl was "possessed with a spirit of divination." In Greek, the word "divination" is "Python." Python was a snake in a Greek myth. Many people believed this mythical snake controlled a priestess at the temple in Delphi, Greece. The people believed this snake was killed by a Greek god named Apollo, whose spirit then controlled the priestess. She acted strangely and muttered, and people believed she could tell what would happen in the future. She was in a trance—some thought either from vapors or from chewing mind-altering leaves. The young girl in Philippi was mentally unbalanced and may also have been drugged, like the priestess.

Here, the King James Version says this girl was "soothsaying," which means "telling the future."

The term "most high God" was used by both Gentiles and Jews. *Gentiles* used the term for Zeus—greatest of the many Greek gods they worshiped. So when the girl used this name to describe what Paul worshiped, it's possible people thought he believed in Zeus. Paul would not have wanted people to think this. Paul was teaching about the power of the one God, who is all good. *Jews* used this term for the one God. So people might have thought Paul was preaching about the Jewish faith. In a Roman city like Philippi, the idea that Paul was trying to convert Romans to the Jewish faith would have upset the Roman leaders. (See **Roman Empire** on page 50.)

One day in Philippi, Paul and his friends were on their way to the river to pray and worship God, when a young girl met them. This girl had a mental problem. She acted strangely, shouting out and perhaps even mumbling at times. The people believed she was controlled by a spirit, and they thought this was a good thing. They believed she could tell them what was going to happen in the future. This girl was the slave of men who used her to make money. People paid them to hear the girl tell about their future. For many days, this girl followed Paul and his friends wherever they went, screaming, "These men are the servants of the most high God! They show us how we can be saved!"

Paul cared deeply about this young girl. He was also troubled because people believed spirits were real and had power over her. He knew there is only one Spirit who is God and that He is always in control and gives only good. He knew that by understanding this, Jesus had healed people with mental illness.

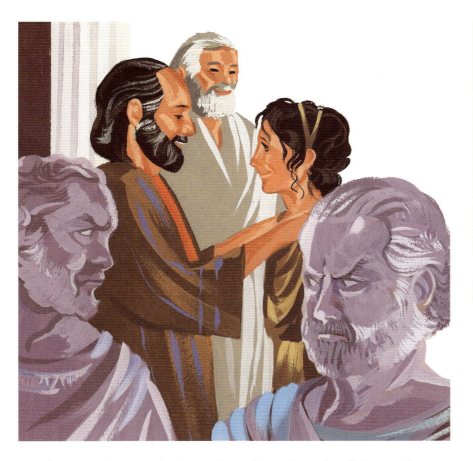

Name of Jesus Christ: See page 13.

This was a brave action to take. The girl's owners would no longer be able to make money from her and would be very angry with Paul.

See John 8:32.

WHAT CAN YOU DO?

What if someone tries to keep others from listening to your good ideas? You can know that everyone is controlled by God. God, who is good, is the only power. He is always showing you and others what is best to do. And you can be brave and stand up to anything that is not good.

Paul turned toward the girl and said to the false evil spirits, "I command you in the **name of Jesus Christ** to come out of her." Paul knew that spirits weren't real—that they were only wrong thinking. He knew that this thinking had to be cast out—or gotten rid of. Then, the truth about this young girl as the spiritual child of God could be seen. Jesus had said, "You shall know the truth and the truth will make you free." Paul was saying that he was casting out this wrong thinking through Jesus' name—which means through the same power and authority of Jesus— through the power of God.

Right away the girl was free! Paul had proved that God is the only Spirit. How thankful the girl must have been—and how eager to learn more about Jesus and how he healed.

Wait on the Lord: be of good courage, and he shall strengthen thine heart.

Psalm 27:14

Paul did not speak out to the girl right away. He was listening to God's good thoughts so that he would be ready to speak out at the right time. We can know that God shows us just when to do something. We can pray—knowing God is good and guides us. We can listen to God's messages and then bravely do what is right. God is always with us, helping us each step of the way.

Paul Restores Eutychus to Life

Acts 20:6-12

Saul/Paul: See page 8.

Followers who traveled with Paul at different periods during this time were: **Silas, Luke, Timothy, Aristarchus,** and others. See page 9.

After healing a girl in Philippi (see "Paul Heals Young Girl of Mental Illness" on page 42) and before the healing in this story, Paul taught and healed in many regions: Palestine, Syria, Galatia, Phrygia, Asia, Macedonia, Illyricum, Achaia (Greece) (Acts 17:1–Acts 20:6; Romans 15:18, 19). Paul wrote to the followers in Corinth, which was in Achaia, reminding them of the healings he had done there (II Corinthians 12:12). Healing was natural to him everywhere he went.

Paul had healed a young girl in Philippi. From there, he left to take his healing message to people in other cities and regions. Sometimes other followers of Jesus traveled with him. ■ On one of his trips, Paul went to Greece and Macedonia and then sailed to the city of Troas. ■

On the first day of the week, **Jesus' followers gathered** in an upstairs room of a house to pray and have a meal together.

Paul had been in Troas all week, but he was leaving the next day, and they wouldn't see him again. So they were eager to hear him talk once more about Jesus **Christ**—his life, his teachings, and his healings. Paul spent as much time as he could with them—talking late into the night.

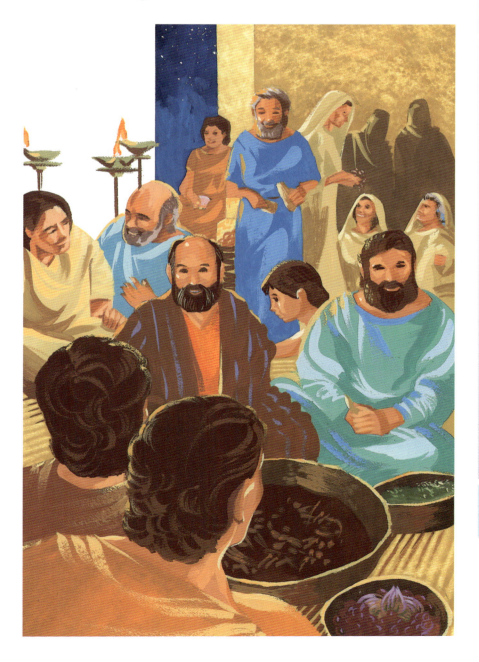

Sunday was the first day of the week according to the Jews. This day had special meaning for Jesus' followers because it was the day that his resurrection had taken place. The followers met on Sundays to eat and worship together. These gatherings were held in the evening because Sunday was a workday for them.

Church: See page 29.

Once a week the early followers of Jesus came together to share a simple meal. Anyone could come— rich or poor, master or slave. Those who could, brought food and in this way helped feed the followers who were poor. The main purpose of the meal was not eating but being together to pray and learn more about Jesus' teachings. Bread was broken, or torn into pieces, and passed around to be used for dipping into the food. After the meal, another prayer was shared. Sometimes the followers sang hymns or someone preached. These meals have been called "love feasts," "feasts of charity," or *agape*—the Greek word for "love"—because the gatherings were loving and joyous. The love feast helped followers feel they were a family. And it reminded them of the last meal the disciples ate with Jesus before he was crucified.

Messiah/Christ: See page 3.

A young boy named Eutychus was sitting on a window sill listening to Paul. Many oil lamps were lit, and the room was probably very warm. Because of this and the late hour—it was around midnight—Eutychus fell sound asleep. Suddenly, he tumbled out of the third-story window to the ground. People rushed down the stairs to help him. When they picked him up, they found he was dead.

Paul went down to Eutychus, too. He bent over him, and, holding him in his arms, said to the others, "Don't be worried or sad. His life is in him." Paul had faith in God's love and care for Eutychus and knew that God is the only power. He trusted God so completely that he left Eutychus and went back upstairs with the followers. He knew that life was more powerful than death even though death seemed so real to everyone else.

Upstairs, Paul ate with the followers and talked with them for a very long time. He probably helped them understand why he had said Eutychus was alive when they believed he was dead. Paul may have talked to them about having faith in God's power. Perhaps he told them how Jesus had brought himself and others back to life. He probably discussed his own healings, including the time men threw stones at him and left him for dead. He had been healed of his injuries through spiritual power. Paul certainly had many wonderful proofs of how the Holy Spirit—the truth about God as the only power and presence—had helped and healed.

When the sun came up, Paul left to continue his trip. The followers went to Eutychus and found that he was alive, just as Paul had said he was. They led this young boy away and were so comforted to see him brought back to life. What a wonderful example to them of God's great power! Paul had proved to them what Jesus proved in his resurrection—life is more powerful than death. And they had seen it with their own eyes!

To be carnally minded is death; but to be spiritually minded is life and peace.

Romans 8:6

Paul was very spiritually minded—filled with the understanding and power of God. So it was natural for him to understand that Eutychus was God's spiritual child, rather than to focus on his material body. When Eutychus died, Paul didn't accept that he was dead. His thought was filled with the good that God gives, including eternal life. And this spiritual mindedness was powerful—it brought Eutychus back to life. Every day, we can learn more about God who is Spirit and depend on Him to help and heal us. As we learn and grow spiritually, we'll understand more and more that God is definitely more powerful than death.

WHAT CAN YOU DO?

Those who were listening to Paul believed that Eutychus was dead. But Paul refused to accept this. He knew in his heart what God knew—that Eutychus was God's spiritual child—full of life and energy. You can take steps every day to see more and more of God's all-power. You can deny what is not like God and accept only what is good. By taking a stand for life and happiness and health and safety, you will grow in your spiritual understanding of God and His power over death.

Paul Heals Himself of Snakebite

Acts 28:1-6

Saul/Paul: See page 8.

Jerusalem: See page 11.

Roman Empire: All the lands around the Mediterranean Sea were part of the Roman Empire, ruled by an emperor. Romans made laws, collected taxes, built roads, and stationed soldiers to keep the peace.

Luke and **Aristarchus:** See page 9.

Paul had brought a boy named Eutychus back to life in Troas. Then, he left that city to go to **Jerusalem.** While he was there, some Jews from Asia said he had done something wrong. They stirred up other Jews against him and even tried to kill him.

The **Romans** arrested Paul for starting trouble and took him to another city where he'd be safe. There, they put him on trial. Paul was a Roman citizen and asked to be tried by the emperor. So he was put on a ship to Rome. Two of his friends went with him. ■

It was a hard trip because the sea was stormy and wild. The ship was beaten with high waves and was blown off its course.

After fourteen days, it was wrecked near an island. In the middle of this storm, Paul had given everyone a comforting message from God. He told them that no one would be harmed—and no one was! Everyone made it to shore.

WHAT CAN YOU DO?

Have you ever been in a very bad storm and been afraid? The storm Paul was in was so bad that the ship was wrecked. But Paul was always so sure of God's love and care that fear couldn't find any place in his thoughts. His calm, clear thinking was a prayer that kept him—and his fellow shipmates—safe. Paul knew that God can help no matter how scary the situation. You can know this, too. God's goodness is with you now and always. No storm can scare you when your thoughts are filled with God's all-power and love.

After bringing Eutychus back to life in Troas (see "Paul Restores Eutychus to Life" on page 46) and before his healing in this story, Paul first traveled to Jerusalem, making stops along the way. Some of the regions he visited on this trip were: Asia, Lycia, Phenicia (Phenice), and Palestine. After this trip, the Roman leaders in Caesarea sent Paul to Rome as a prisoner. The ship stopped at Phenicia (Phenice), and Lycia (Acts 20:13–27:1). Paul was filled with the Holy Spirit—the great power and understanding of God. Everywhere he went he taught about God's love and care for everyone. It would have been perfectly natural for healings to result from what he lived and taught. Earlier, in his letter to the Romans, Paul told of the mighty healings he had done through the power of the Spirit, from Jerusalem all the way to Illyricum (Romans 15:18,19).

Here, the King James Version refers to these people as "barbarous people." This didn't mean the people were wild or uncivilized. The Greek term means "foreigners." Other translations use the word "natives."

Here, the King James Version says "vengeance" would not let him live. The Greek word for "vengeance" is the name of the goddess of justice. These people believed that this Greek goddess would not allow Paul to live.

When Paul and the others got to land, they discovered that the island was Melita. ■ The people who lived on the island ■ were very kind. It was rainy and cold, and they welcomed Paul and the others by making a fire to warm them.

Paul helped keep the fire going by gathering a bundle of sticks. As he was laying the sticks on the fire, a poisonous snake slithered out, bit his hand, and held on tightly. When the people who lived on the island saw the snake hanging from Paul's hand, they said to each other, "Even though this man escaped from the shipwreck, he must be a murderer, and he won't be allowed to live." ■ These people believed that when something bad happened to someone, it meant that person had done something wrong—and was being punished for it by one of their gods.

Paul's great faith in God made him strong and fearless. Even a wild storm, a shipwreck, and a poisonous snake didn't scare him. He knew that God was with him—keeping him safe every moment. Paul knew deep down that God would help him no matter what happened. We can be like Paul and face scary times with trust in God. We can feel His love all around us and be unafraid.

Paul wasn't afraid of the snake. He knew that God is good and all powerful—always taking care of him. Therefore, nothing—not even that snake—had any power to hurt him. He just shook the snake off into the fire.

Those who lived on the island looked to see if Paul would swell up or if he'd suddenly fall down and die from the snakebite. When they could see that nothing bad had happened to him, they decided he was not a murderer. Instead, they thought he must be a god. These people did not understand how Paul's healing happened, but they realized that he was healed through a power that was not human.

What a good step this was for these people to begin to see what the power and understanding of the one God can do!

Paul Heals Publius of Illness

Acts 28:7-10

Saul/Paul: See page 8.

Luke and **Aristarchus:** See page 9.

The King James Version says that this man was sick of "a fever and of a bloody flux." This meant he suffered from dysentery, a serious stomach disease that often lasted several months and frequently resulted in death.

On the way to Rome as a prisoner, **Paul** had been shipwrecked near the island of Melita. There he was healed of a snakebite. The ruler of the island was a man named Publius. He was very kind to Paul and **his friends** and invited them to stay at his house for three days. At that time, Publius' father was very sick.

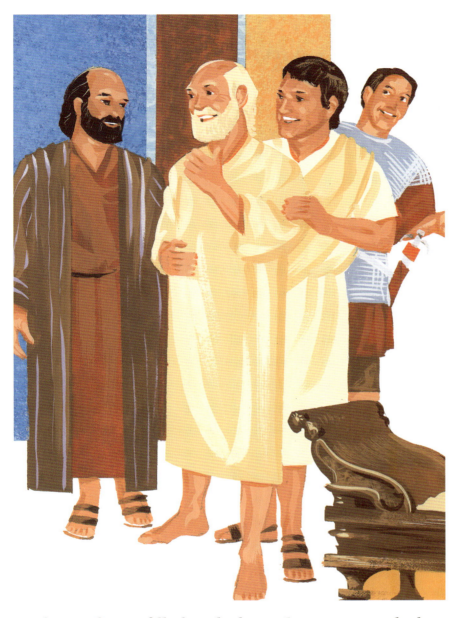

Holy Spirit: See page 4.

Messiah/Christ: See page 3.

Laying on of Hands/Healing by Touch: See page 13.

WHAT CAN YOU DO?

Have you ever felt unhappy about something in your life and thought you couldn't do anything about it? If so, remember Paul. He was a prisoner of the Romans. The ship he was on was shipwrecked, and then he was stranded on an island. But no matter how bad things were, he knew that God loved him and always took care of him. You can know God loves you, too. Wherever you are, whatever has happened to you, you are never alone. God will help you and comfort you. Nothing is impossible with God's help!

Paul was always filled with the **Holy Spirit**—with the spiritual understanding of God's power. He was ready to help and heal—just as **Christ** Jesus had been. So he went to this man and prayed. He **put his hand on him,** which must have made him feel loved and cared for. In his prayer Paul knew that God created this man to be His perfect, spiritual, healthy child. He knew God kept him that way. Right away, the man was healed. How happy he must have been to be well again! The news of this wonderful healing spread quickly around the island.

Disciple/Apostle: See page 10.

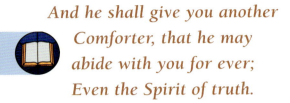

And he shall give you another Comforter, that he may abide with you for ever; Even the Spirit of truth.

John 14:16, 17

Jesus promised his followers that after he was gone, their Father would give them the Comforter or Holy Spirit—the truth that God who is good is the only power and presence. Paul's heart and mind were filled with this understanding, and it enabled him to heal. When he was faced with something that wasn't good, he didn't accept it as the truth. He knew that God was in control and that His love and power were always with him. We have this same Spirit of truth. God takes care of us every moment, bringing infinite good into our lives. Jesus knew it, Paul knew it, and we can know it, too.

Soon all the other sick people on the island of Melita were coming to Paul—and they were healed, too! For the next three months, Paul and his shipmates stayed on the island. Paul must have spent many hours telling the islanders about Jesus' life and teachings—and healing those who were sick.

And when the new ship was ready to leave for Rome, these people shared what they had with Paul. The islanders made sure that he and the others had everything they needed for the trip. They must have loved this great **apostle** who had shown them a new way to think and live and heal. They wanted him to know how grateful they were for all he had done. They would never forget him. Think what it meant to them to learn from Paul that the Holy Spirit—spiritual power—was within them, too. And with this power, they would be able to continue Paul's wonderful healing work!

Bibliography

GENERAL

Arlandson, James Malcolm. *Women, Class, and Society in Early Christianity.* Peabody: Hendrickson, 1997.

Brown, Raymond E. *An Introduction to The New Testament.* New York: Doubleday, 1997.

Buckmaster, Henrietta. *Paul: A Man Who Changed the World.* New York: McGraw-Hill, 1965.

Conybeare, The Rev. W. J., and Howson, The Very Rev. J. S. *The Life and Epistles of St. Paul.* Grand Rapids: W. B. Eerdmans, 1954.

Deen, Edith. *All of The Women of The Bible.* San Francisco: Harper & Row, 1955.

Eddy, Mary Baker. *Prose Works other than Science and Health with Key to the Scriptures.* Boston: The First Church of Christ, Scientist, 1953.

Eddy, Mary Baker. *Science and Health with Key to the Scriptures.* Boston: The First Church of Christ, Scientist, 1934.

Goodspeed, Edgar J. *Paul.* Philadelphia: John C. Winston, 1947.

Greece and Rome: Builders of Our World. Edited by Merle Severy. Washington, D.C.: National Geographic Society, 1968.

Groser, Audrey. *Morning Glory—the story of the first Christians and their risen Christ.* Lincs, England: Autumn House, 2000.

Harris, Stephen L. *The New Testament, A Student's Introduction.* Mountain View: Mayfield, 1995.

Kee, Howard Clark., Young, Franklin W., Froehlich, Karlfried. *Understanding The New Testament.* Englewood Cliffs: Prentice-Hall, 1965.

Maier, Paul L. *In The Fullness of Time.* San Francisco: Harper, 1991.

Meinardus, Otto F. A. *St. Paul in Greece.* Athens: Lycabettus Press, 1977.

Miller, Rex. *I, Paul.* Granada Hills: The Friendly Shop, 1988.

Robinson, Russell D. *Teaching the Scriptures.* Milwaukee: Bible Study, 1993.

Sergio, Lisa. *Jesus and Woman.* McLean: EPM, 1975.

Shepard, J. W. *The Life and Letters of St. Paul.* Grand Rapids: W. B. Eerdmans, 1950.

BIBLES

Amplified Bible. Grand Rapids: Zondervan, 1965.

Gaus, Andy. *The Unvarnished New Testament.* Grand Rapids: Phanes, 1991.

Good News Bible, The Bible in Today's English Version. Nashville: Thomas Nelson, 1976.

The Living Bible. Wheaton: Tyndale, 1976.

Hastings, Selina. *The Children's Illustrated Bible.* New York: DK, 1994.

The Holy Bible. Authorized King James Version. New York: Oxford University.

The Illustrated Family Bible. Edited by Claude-Bernard Costecalde. New York: DK, 1997.

New Jerusalem Bible. New York: Doubleday, 1990.

New Living Translation. Wheaton: Tyndale, 1996.

New International Version. Wheaton: Tyndale, 1984.

Bibliography

Peterson, Eugene H. *The Message: The Bible in Contemporary Language.* Colorado Springs: Navpress, 2002.

Phillips, J.B. *The New Testament in Modern English.* New York: Macmillan, 1972.

DICTIONARIES AND CONCORDANCES

The Anchor Bible Dictionary. Edited by David Noel Freedman. New York: Doubleday, 1992.

Dictionary of Judaism in the Biblical Period. Edited by Jacob Neusner. Peabody: Hendrickson, 1966.

Dictionary of the Bible. Edited by James Hastings. New York: Charles Scribner's Sons, 1963.

HarperCollins Bible Dictionary. San Francisco: Harper, 1996.

Illustrated Dictionary of Bible Life and Times. Pleasantville: Reader's Digest, 1997.

International Standard Bible Encyclopedia Electronic Edition STEP Files. Parsons Technology, 1998.

The Interpreter's Dictionary of the Bible. Edited by G. A. Buttrick. Nashville: Abingdon, 1962.

Quick Verse for Windows Version 5.0c. Cedar Rapids: Parsons Technology, 1992-1998.

Holman Bible Dictionary. Edited by Trent C. Butler.

International Standard Bible Encyclopedia. Edited by James Orr, 1998.

Strong, James. *The Exhaustive Concordance of The Bible.* Nashville: Abingdon, 1980.

Thayer, Joseph H. *Thayer's Greek-English Lexicon of the New Testament.* Grand Rapids: Baker, 1977.

COMMENTARIES

Barclay, William. *The Daily Study Bible.* Philadelphia: Westminster, 1975.

A Commentary on The Holy Bible. Edited by Rev. J.R. Dummelow. New York: Macmillan, 1939.

The Expositor's Bible Commentary. Edited by Frank E. Gaebelein. Grand Rapids: Zondervan, 1984.

Harper's Bible Commentary. Edited by James L. Mays. San Francisco: Harper & Row, 1988.

The Interpreter's Bible. Nashville: Abingdon, 1982.

The Interpreter's One-Volume Commentary on the Bible. Edited by Charles M. Laymon. Nashville: Abingdon, 1971.

Bibliography

JFB Commentary on The Whole Bible. Edited by Robert Jamieson, A. E. Fausset, David Brown. Grand Rapids: Zondervan, 1961.

Henry, Matthew. *Matthew Henry's Commentary on the Whole Bible*. New York: Fleming H. Revell.

The New Interpreter's Bible in Twelve Volumes. Edited by Leander E. Keck. Nashville: Abingdon, 1995.

Stern, David S. *Jewish New Testament Commentary*. Clarksville, MD: Jewish New Testament Publications, Inc. 1995.

The Tyndale New Testament Commentaries. Edited by Canon Leon Morris. Grand Rapids: William B. Eerdmans, 1985.

Williams, David, J. *New International Biblical Commentary—Volume on Acts*. Peabody: Hendrickson, 1990.

The Wycliffe Bible Commentary. Edited by Everett G. Harrison. Nashville: Southwestern, 1962.

ATLASES

Atlas of the Bible Lands. Edited by Harry Thomas Frank. Maplewood, NJ: Hammond, 1990.

Oxford Bible Atlas. Edited by Herbert G. May. London: Oxford University, 1976.

DAILY LIFE IN BIBLE TIMES

After Jesus. Edited by Gayla Visalli. Pleasantville: Reader's Digest, 1992.

Connolly, Peter. *Living in the Time of Jesus of Nazareth*. Israel: Steimatzky, 1983.

Gower, Ralph. *The New Manners and Customs of Bible Times*. Chicago: Moody Press, 1987.

Great People of the Bible and How They Lived. Pleasantville: Reader's Digest, 1974.

Harper's Encyclopedia of Bible Life. Madeleine S. and J. Lane Miller. Edison: Castle, 1978.

Jesus and His Times. Edited by Kaari Ward. Pleasantville: Reader's Digest, 1987.

Keyes, Nelson Beecher. *Reader's Digest Story of the Bible World*. Pleasantville: Reader's Digest, 1962.

Thompson, J. A. *Handbook of Life in Bible Times*. Madison: Inter-Varsity, 1986.

Index to Bible Verses

With this index, you will be able to find Bible verses in the stories and sidebars. In some cases, the Bible verses are paraphrased, rather than quoted or referenced. Bible books, chapters, and verses below are in the left column and in bold type. Page numbers are to the right of the verses. Page numbers in bold type indicate this verse is the subject of a sidebar.

Index to "What Can YOU Do?" Sidebars

Below are listed the "concerns" addressed in sidebars.

General Index

General Index

fearless/without fear, 36,53
  see also brave
  see also courage
fellowship/family, 26,47
fever, 54
forgive, 7,26,27

Galatia, 1,5,9,42,46
gate, 12,14
Gentiles, 8,**25**,36,38,39,42-44
god/gods, 40,44,52,53
  see also myth
Godlike, 4,25,29,34
gospel/good news, 3,8,9,10,17,
  25,29,41
grateful/thanks/thankful, 14,20,
  36,39,41,45,47,56
Greece/Achaia, 1,5,9,46

Hand, 13,24,34,55
  see also "laying on of hands"
health/healthy, 10,12,30,49,55
high priest/chief priests, 21,25
Holy Ghost, 4,10
  see Holy Spirit
Holy Spirit, 3-11,16,18,20,26,27,
  28,35,36,38,52,55,56
hope, 31

Iconium, 36-38
Illyricum, 1,46,52
image/likeness, 3,4,12,14,17,20,
  22,36,39,41
impure, 12
injuries, 40,49

Jerusalem, 4-8,**11**,12,18,19,21,
  25,28,29,32,38,42,50,52
Jesus, 3-6,8,10-19,21-27,29-38,
  41,42,44,45,47,49,54-56
Jews/Jewish, 3,8,11,12,17,18,
    19-21,23-25,33,36,38,43,44,
    47,50
  burial customs, **31**
  cleanness, laws of, 15
  fasting, 23
  leaders, 17,21
  mourning customs, **33**
John, 5,**6**,10-15
John Mark, 8,**9**,37
Joppa, 31-34
Judas, 10,11

Kill/get rid of, 7,17,21,35,37,38,
  40,41,50
kindness/care/love, 4,7,8,10,11,
  13,15,17-20,22,26,27,29-31,
  33-36,38,39,41,44,47,48,
  51-53,55,56
know/knew, 3,4,14,17,20,26,27,
  30,32-34,36,39,41,44,45,48,
  49,51,53,55,56
  see also pray/prayer
  see also thinking,thought
  see also understand/
    understood

Lame, 5,6,7,8,10-15,18,20,37-39
law/laws (Jewish)
  cleanness, 12,15
laying on of hands, 13,24,34,55
life, restored to, 3,5,31-34,46-49
listen, 4,17,19,23,25,29,33,38,
  39,45
lonely/alone, 10,33,55
Lord, **22**,24,25
love/care/kindness, 4,7,8,10,11,
  13,15,17-20,22,26,27,29-31,
  33-36,38,39,41,44,47,48,
  51-53,55,56
love feast/*agape*, **47**
Luke, **9**,31,43,46,50
Lycaonia, 38,42
Lycia, 52
Lydda, 29,32
Lydia, **43**
Lystra, 9,38-41

Macedonia, 1,9,43,46
map, about the, 1
Matthias, 10,11
meal, 27,47
Mediterranean Sea, 50,51
Melita, 51-56
mental illness, 42-45
Messiah, **3**,11,19
most high God, **44**
mourning customs, **33**
Mysia, 42
myth, 44
  see also god/gods

Name of Jesus Christ, **13**,45
name, Paul, **35**,37

Opposition to Paul, **38**,40

Palestine, 1,38,42,46,52
Pamphylia, 1,38,42
paralysis/paralyzed/palsy, 3,5,
  6,7,18,**20**,28-30

Paul, 1,5,**8**,9,13,35-56
  see also Saul
Paul's name, 8,**35**,37
peace, 19,34
Pentecost, 4,5,**11**,12,16,18,26,28
perfect, 4,10,14,20,27,30,39,55
Peter, 5,**6**,10-15,28-30,31-34
Phenicia/Phenice/Phoenicia, 1,
  42,52
Philip, 5,**7**,18-20
Philippi, 43-45
Phrygia, 42,46
Pisidia, 38,42
power, 3-6,8-11,13,16-20,26,
  28-34,36-39,41,42,44,45,48,
  49,51-53,55,56
pray/prayer/praying, 4-7,9,12,
  19,24,30,31,34,36,37,41,
  43-45,47,51,55
  see also know/knew
  see also think/thought
  see also understood/
    understand(ing)
Publius, 54-56
pure/purification, 15,25-27,
  29,34
Python, 44

Repent, 11
restored to life, 3,5,31-34,46-49
  see also risen/raised/rose from
    death
resurrection, 4,6,10,22,32,47,49
risen/raised/rose from death, 4,
  11,31,41
  see also restored to life
Rome/Romans/Roman Empire,
  1,5,8,9,35,37,44,**50**,52,54,56

Sabbath, 21
sackcloth, 33
sad, 48
safe/safety, 34,41,49,51,53
saints, 16,25,29,34
Samaria/Samaritans, 6,7,19,
  20,42
Sanhedrin, 21
Saron, **30**
Saul, 7,**8**,21-27,35,37
  see also Paul
sea, 51
shipwreck, 51,53,54
sick/sickness, 3-5,12,14,20,22,26,
  28,32,36,54-56
Silas, **9**,42,43,46
sin, 3,4,7,22,26
sisters, 16
snake, 44,52,53

snakebite, 1,5,8,50-53
Solomon's Porch, **15**
soothsaying, 44
spirit/spirits, 44,45
Spirit of God, 3,4
Spirit of truth, 4,5,27,56
Stephen, 1,5,7,16,17
stomach disease/dysentery, 1,5,
  8,54
stones/stoning/stoned, 7,8,
  40-42,49
storm, 51,53
strong/strength/strengthen, 4,
  25,30,36,41,53
Sunday, 47
superstitious, 40
swell up, 53
synagogue, 3,**21**
Syria, 1,37,38,42,46

Tabitha/Dorcas, 31-34
teach/teaching/taught, 4-12,
  15-17,19,20,25-27,29,36-38,
  41-43,52,56
Temple, 6,11,**12**,14,15,17,19,32
thanks/thankful/grateful, 14,20,
  36,39,41,45,47,56
Thessalonica, 9
think/thinking/thought, 12,30,
  51,56
  see also know/knew
  see also pray/prayer
  see also understood/
    understand
Timothy, **9**,43,46
touch/touched, 12,**13**,24,26
Troas, 9,43,46-49,50,52
trust/trusted/trusting, 6,9,13,20,
  30,34,35,39,48,53
truth/truths/true, 1,3-5,10,14,17,
  27,35-37,41,45,49,56

Unclean/clean, **12**,15
unclean spirits, 20
understood/understand(ing),
  1,3,4,11,13,15-17,20,22,26,
  27,29,41,44,49,52,53,55,56
  see also know/knew
  see also pray/prayer
unkind, 27,36
upper room/upstairs room, **31**,
  33,47

Way, the, 16,21,22
widows, 6,33,34
worry, 48
worship/worshiped, 3,17,19,25,
  40,44

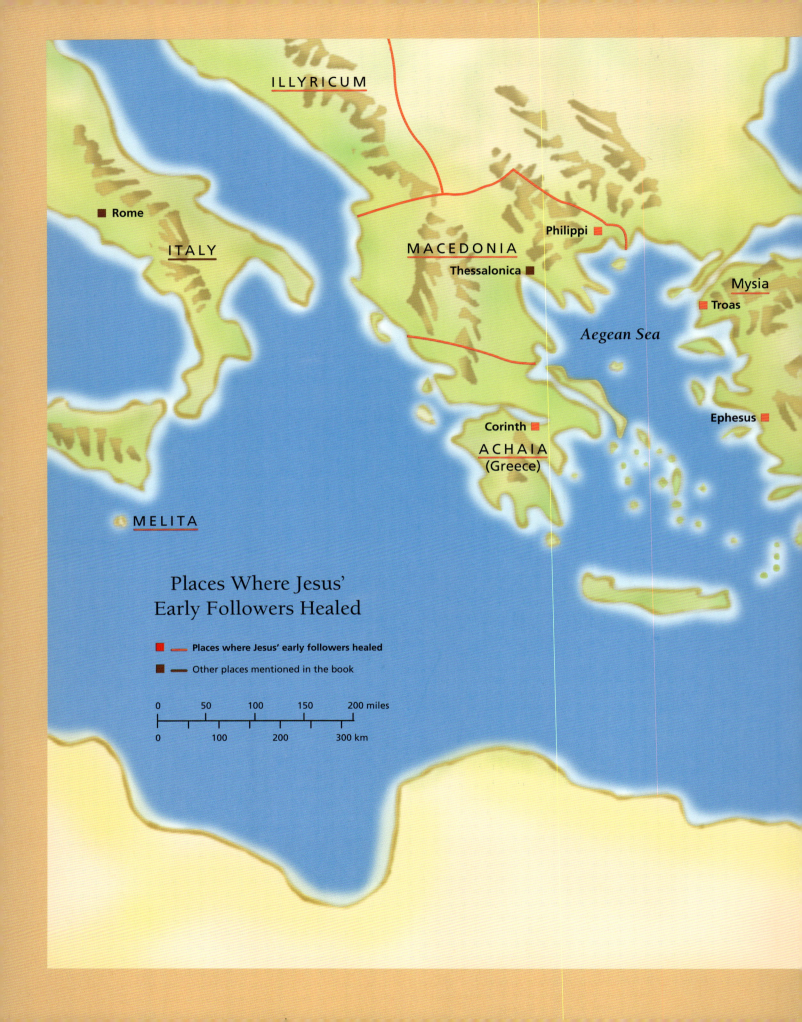

ILLYRICUM

Rome

ITALY

MACEDONIA

Philippi

Thessalonica

Mysia

Troas

Aegean Sea

Corinth

ACHAIA
(Greece)

Ephesus

MELITA

Places Where Jesus'
Early Followers Healed

Places where Jesus' early followers healed

Other places mentioned in the book

0	50	100	150	200 miles
0	100	200	300 km	